Reid Hoffman and
LinkedIn

INTERNET BIOGRAPHIES™

Reid Hoffman and
LinkedIn

ANN BYERS

Rosen
PUBLISHING®
New York

Published in 2014 by The Rosen Publishing Group, Inc.
29 East 21st Street, New York, NY 10010

First Edition

Library of Congress Cataloging-in-Publication Data

Byers, Ann.
Reid Hoffman and Linkedin/Ann Byers.
    p. cm.—(Internet biographies)
Includes bibliographical references and index.
ISBN 978-1-4488-9524-3 (library binding)
1. Hoffman, Reid. 2. LinkedIn (Electronic resource) 3. Linkedin (Firm)
4. Business networks—United States. 5. Webmasters—United States—
Biography. 6. Businesspeople—United States—Biography. 7. Online
social networks. I. Title.
HD69.S8B94 2014
381'.142092—dc23
[B]

2012036278

Manufactured in the United States of America

CPSIA Compliance Information: Batch #S13YA: For further information, contact Rosen Publishing, New York,
New York, at 1-800-237-9932.

Contents

INTRODUCTION

The young man did not really expect a response to his message. He knew that Reid Hoffman was one of the most sought after investors in the Internet industry and one of the busiest. Hoffman had launched LinkedIn in 2003, barely a year earlier, and it was already on its way to more than a million users. Why would he respond to Cyriac Roeding, a relatively unknown man from Germany?

But he did respond! Not only did he answer, but he also invited Roeding to have breakfast with him the next time he was in Silicon Valley in California. When Roeding took him up on his offer, Hoffman extended another. Hoffman and Roeding continued to meet whenever Roeding could, which was two or three times each year.

Hoffman responded to Roeding because of a moral principle he holds dear: everyone should do something that's not for himself or herself. It's one of three values that are very important to him—having a personal impact for good. He wants to be involved in enterprises that make the world a better place. That is the reason why he has invested in well over one hundred new companies, helping them get off the ground. That is why he serves on the boards of many organizations. He enjoys helping people do good things.

Another of his three top values is relationships. He started LinkedIn precisely to help people, specifically

Reid Hoffman is a big man who makes a big impression wherever he goes. He is pictured here at a business conference in his typically casual attire.

people in a professional context, form, improve, and make use of their relationships. The tagline of the company is "Relationships matter." The high value Hoffman places on people is the reason why he begins every business day with breakfast with an associate or someone who wants his help and ends with dinner with someone else. It is why he packs his days—often from eight in the morning until six or seven at night—with appointments with budding entrepreneurs who ask him for advice, many of whom are people he has never met, like Cyriac Roeding. He stays connected with his many contacts and friends with five smartphones, two Macs, one PC, an iPad, and an Android tablet.

Roeding had formed a successful mobile advertising company, but he had dreams for other kinds of businesses, and Reid Hoffman is all about nurturing dreams, especially big dreams. His third value is scale—bigness. Hoffman is interested in ideas that touch huge numbers of people—not hundreds, but millions. LinkedIn adds a million new members every week. Roeding had ideas of the same scale.

The two men kept talking for five years. Roeding moved to California and eventually started a new company called Shopkick. He was able to launch his dream because Hoffman invested money in it. As a member of Shopkick's board, Hoffman continued to encourage, guide, and support the young business. When he joined an investment firm, Hoffman secured money from that firm for Shopkick as well.

Roeding's story is not unusual. Hundreds of aspiring entrepreneurs like Roeding have received advice, encouragement, and start-up funds from Reid Hoffman. All of his actions and decisions are guided by three principles: making the greatest impact for good, valuing relationships, and working toward massive scale. Hoffman has frequently said he would like society to be a better place because he has "been there." Many, such as Roeding, would say it is.

CHAPTER 1

A Radical Start

Reid Hoffman did not acquire his values by accident. The principles he lives by, especially the desire to make an impact for good, have been part of his family's value system for generations. His great, great, great grandfather taught at the University of Indiana in the decades before and after the Civil War, when African Americans had very few opportunities. When the university enrolled its first African American in 1882 and the community denied him housing, Hoffman's ancestor took him into his own home so that he could receive a college education.

Hoffman's grandparents were also active in promoting civil rights for African Americans. In the 1960s, when African Americans were being scared away from voting booths and civil rights workers were being killed, Hoffman's grandfather piloted a small plane to fly two activists from his home in California to Mississippi, where they guarded the polling places so that everyone could vote. Although his grandfather had served proudly in the navy during World War II and in Korea, he was against the U.S. military involvement in Vietnam. Both he and his wife, Hoffman's grandmother, marched in protests against the war. Both were graduates of the University of California, Berkeley, where activism and demonstrations were common.

About the time his grandparents were marching against the Vietnam War, in 1967, Reid Garrett Hoffman was born in Stanford, California. His father and mother were much like his grandparents. His father had graduated from Stanford and practiced public service law;

Protests against racial discrimination in the 1960s often drew thousands of people, such as at this Black Panther demonstration in Los Angeles, California. His activist parents sometimes took young Reid to civil rights demonstrations.

his mother had studied environmental law at Berkeley. They, too, marched through tear gas at demonstrations, carrying Reid, their only child. Like his grandparents, his mother and father were also passionate about civil rights. His father sometimes slept at the headquarters of the Black Panthers, an African American activist group, "in case the police kicked down the door," Hoffman told *Wired* magazine, "because the police were less likely to shoot a white person."

Discussions in Hoffman's childhood home in Berkeley were about what was right and wrong and what individuals could and should do about injustice. As early as age twelve, Hoffman and his young friends drew up a plan for how they would rule the world and make it a better place. He learned the value of making an impact for good early in life.

LOVE OF GAMES

Also fairly early in life he developed a love for games. Not the typical childhood games, but role-playing games that involved creating characters and playing the parts of those characters. Hoffman was always fascinated with how people think and interact. When he was ten, his babysitter showed him a new game that had been on the market only three years and was fast becoming popular: *Dungeons and Dragons*. It was a role-playing game and Hoffman loved it.

Later one of his friends told him about a similar game called *RuneQuest*. The new game had been created and produced by a company called Chaosium, which was located not far from where Hoffman lived. The boy became obsessed with the game. He spent every spare moment playing it and even started hanging out at the Chaosium office. But when he played the game, he found some instructions that he saw as flaws in the design of the game. He figured he knew how to fix them, how to make the game better. He made notes and suggestions on his copy of the rule sheet for the game. Then twelve-year-old Reid Hoffman took his ideas and his notes to Chaosium's headquarters.

On that Friday, Steve Perrin was in the office. The boy probably didn't know that Perrin had written the rules for *Dungeons and Dragons* and had created *RuneQuest*. Perrin may have been big in the world of game design, but Hoffman considered himself an expert in game playing. The twelve-year-old handed his marked-up manual to Perrin.

Perrin was a little surprised, but he was impressed with Hoffman's comments on his game. He was in the process of developing new games for the *RuneQuest* system, and he could use this boy's insights to improve his products. He asked him if he would look at the plans he was working on. Hoffman took the manual for the new game home. He worked on it from Friday night all through the

Settlers of Catan

In *Settlers of Catan*, players assume the roles of people coming to the primitive island of Catan. The island has a number of resources—ore, brick, lumber, grain, and wool—and the players use the resources to establish settlements, build cities, and make roads that connect their holdings. Like entrepreneurs in start-up companies, players make business decisions, trade with others, and deal with competition and misfortunes. Just as in real life, one person's moves affect the fates of others.

Since its release in 1995, *Settlers* has become hugely popular; it has sold more than fifteen million copies and has been translated into thirty languages. A number of spinoffs have been produced: expansions of the original board game, a card game, computer versions, games for nearly every type of gaming system, and a novel. It is little wonder that the *Washington Post* compared it to Monopoly, calling it the "board game of our time."

weekend, stopping only to eat and sleep. When he brought it back Monday morning, Perrin paid him for his consulting work. Hoffman's name is listed as one of the authors of *Borderlands*, a *RuneQuest* game produced in 1982.

Games still interest Hoffman, specifically games in which people form relationships and interact. He loves playing *Settlers of Catan*, a German board game that has won a number of international awards. Like *Rune-Quest*, it is a role-playing game. But unlike the earlier product, it is not set in a fantasy world. People accumulate resources, trade commodities, and make decisions about where to place their wealth. It is a game, Hoffman believes, that is very much like starting and running businesses. His friends say he is particularly good at teaching the game to newcomers.

SCHOOL

Perhaps because of his obsession with role-playing games, Hoffman did not do particularly well in school. His grades were merely average, and sometimes he was caught reading science-fiction books in class. Seeking a little adventure of his own, Hoffman decided he wanted to go to high school in Vermont. To a California boy in a city of glass and steel, the idea of living in a dorm on a farm seemed like fun. He could drive oxen through snow-covered woods, learn to be a blacksmith, gather maple syrup, and go cross-country skiing in the Green Mountains. Without telling his parents, he applied to the Putney School, a private boarding school . . . and was accepted. Then he talked his mom and dad into sending him all the way across the country to attend high school.

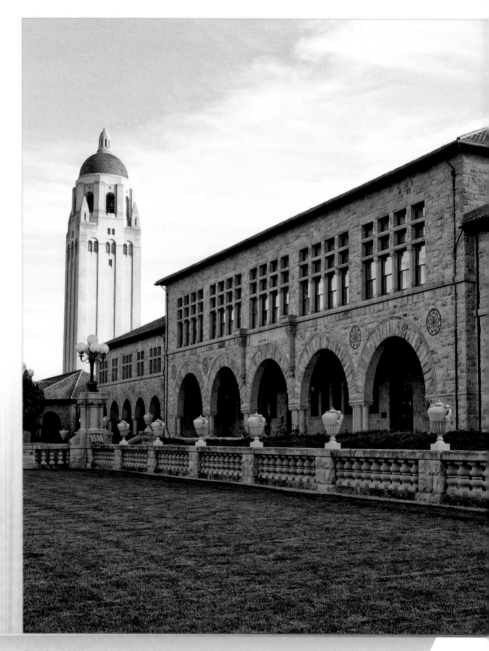

Stanford University, which Hoffman attended, is located between San Francisco and San Jose, California, in the middle of Silicon Valley. It has grown from 555 students in 1891 to well over 15,000 today.

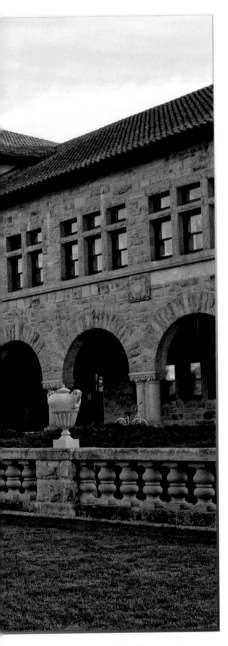

But he returned to California for college. He had done well at Putney, well enough to enroll at Stanford, another very prestigious school, from which his father had graduated and his grandfather had earned a law degree. He earned a master of science degree in symbolic systems. Symbolic systems is the science that studies systems that use symbols to represent information. It examines a natural system (the human mind) and an artificial system (computers). It is a combination of psychology, philosophy, and computer science. Reid Hoffman basically studied the ways people think and communicate and the relationships between people and computers.

One of the relationships he made at Stanford would prove to be important for years to come. Peter Thiel was in one of Hoffman's philosophy classes. Their views on most matters were as different as day and

Marshall Scholarship

The Marshall Scholarship is an expression of friendship and gratitude to the United States from the people of Great Britain. In 1947, England, as well as most of the rest of Europe, was physically and economically devastated as a result of World War II, which had ended two years earlier. U.S. President Harry Truman launched the European Recovery Program that provided billions of dollars in food, fuel, machinery, and technical assistance that got the European nations back on their feet. Under the direction of Secretary of State George Marshall, the Marshall Plan has been credited with saving and rebuilding sixteen countries. In 1953, the British government established the Marshall Scholarship, which permitted twelve "intellectually distinguished" American graduates to study in England. That number was increased over the years to forty. The award strengthens the relationship between the United States and Britain and serves as an enduring thank-you from a grateful friend.

night. They argued for eight hours the first time they met and for many, many hours in the months and years since. They disagreed vehemently, but they always enjoyed the debates. When both men ran for student senate, they decided to join forces, combining their campaigns and running as a team. The joint ticket beat all opponents, and the two have continued as partners and friends to this day.

While at Stanford, Hoffman was one of two students to win the Dinkelspiel Award, a prize given for outstanding contributions to undergraduate education. He also received a Marshall Scholarship. This is an award that went at that time, in 1990, to no more than thirty people. Winners had to be graduating from a U.S. college with a GPA of at least 3.7. The scholarship entitled them to study for two years in England at any university they chose. It covered tuition, books, travel, cost of living, and some other expenses. Hoffman selected Oxford University.

CHANGING COURSE

When Hoffman was at Stanford, many of his friends did volunteer work. Some tutored children in a poorer community not far from the school. One was a young lady named Michelle Yee, who was studying to be a speech pathologist and whom he married about five years after he graduated. As Hoffman watched his friends and his future wife, he thought about what he wanted to do with his life. He asked himself: how can I make a contribution to society that really matters? That is what led him to Oxford. He decided to earn a master's in philosophy. He would become what he called a "public intellectual." He would

Reid Hoffman married his college sweetheart, Michelle Yee. Here, they pose for a picture at Bodega Bay on the California coast in summer 2010.

write books on important topics; that is the way he would impact the world for good.

But after his first year at Oxford, Hoffman's value of working on a large scale began to gnaw at him. Earlier, while his classmates at Stanford were teaching dozens of kids, he had dreamed of doing something that might touch thousands. At Oxford, he realized that if he became a philosopher or a college professor, he might write a wonderful book full of great ideas, but probably no more than sixty people would read it or even know about it. But if he could produce some kind of service that would help people in their daily lives, perhaps millions would benefit. He decided then and there that teaching at a university was not for him. He would make his impact somewhere in the business world.

CHAPTER 2

Plan A: Toward an Internet Start-Up

With his master's degree in philosophy, Hoffman returned to California in 1993. He operated according to what he would later call ABZ planning. Plan A was a job along the career path he wanted, a job he had the skills and abilities to do well. Plan B was a different job, perhaps involving the same career goals. If both plans failed, he would fall back on Plan Z, a safety net. For Hoffman, Plan A was starting his own business.

FIRST ATTEMPT

When he tried to figure out what kind of service he could offer that would make the world a better place, he thought of software. He had studied computer systems in college, so he understood technology. He had some ideas for programs that could help people. But he didn't know whether those ideas would really work. If he created a good software product, how would he sell it? How could he turn it into a business? He didn't know how the world of entrepreneurship—starting businesses—operated.

He did know that beginning a business would take money, and he knew that venture capitalists supplied that money. Venture capitalists are people or companies with money that are willing to risk some of what they have to help new businesses start or expand. They give money to new ventures that look like they might make it big. Hoffman, of course, expected to make it big. Fortunately for him, nearly a third of all venture capitalist investments are made to Silicon Valley companies, and he was living with his grandparents in Los Altos, in the heart of Silicon Valley.

Hoffman found investors in the same way he would find every future business connection: by networking. He asked himself who he knew who might be familiar with the people he wanted to meet. He had friends introduce him to some venture capitalists who might be interested in a technology start-up.

The people he contacted all had the same questions for Hoffman. Had he actually produced any software? Had he shipped software products to any customers? Was he seriously asking them to invest in the business idea of someone with zero experience in that business? Or in any business, for that matter? They told him to work in the industry before trying to start his own software company.

Hoffman didn't mind working for established companies, but his ultimate goal was to start his own. He asked himself how he could get to that goal quickly; what was the fastest way? What was the shortest amount of time he would have to work for someone else before he could be on his own? He came up with a check-off list, he later told *Inc.* magazine: "Need experience designing, need experience in product management, need experience shipping product, need experience in building a team." Once he mastered each of these tasks, he reasoned, he could start a software company.

LEARNING PRODUCT DEVELOPMENT

The first item on Hoffman's to-do list was to learn how to design software. One of the biggest names in software development was Apple Computer, and Hoffman had a connection there. A good friend from his college days had a roommate who worked at Apple. He was able to get Hoffman his first job in the computer industry. He became part of Apple's user experience group.

In user experience, employees design software in ways that make the experience of using it easier or more

fun for the person who would purchase the product. It was
a perfect fit for Hoffman, whose college work was all about
the interactions between people and computers. But it was
not going to get him closer to his goal of starting his own

When Hoffman started at Apple in 1994, the company created the QuickTake
digital camera. Pictures could be viewed only by connecting the camera to a
Macintosh computer by cable.

company. He discovered that designing a product was not as important to a business as figuring out how to market, or sell, that product. What good is a great, well-designed software program if no one needs or wants it? At Apple, marketing was part of product management; each product had its own management department. Hoffman realized he needed to move from user experience to product management. But those jobs required experience that Hoffman didn't have.

So he devised a way to get the experience: he offered to work for free. He selected one of Apple's products—eWorld—and came up with some ideas for improving it. He talked to the person in charge of product management for eWorld and asked if he could explore some possibilities for making the product better. He wrote up his ideas on the side, while he continued to do his regular job. People on the eWorld team looked at what he produced and gave him feedback.

EWorld was an early and rather unsophisticated social networking site, an attempt to establish an online community. The product had a very short life. One reason was that online services were quite new; when Hoffman came to Apple in 1994, probably fewer than five hundred thousand people used the Internet. EWorld was not available to all of them because it worked on only Macintosh computers. Although it was attractive, clever, and easy to use, it was more expensive than other online services.

EWorld debuted in 1994 and shut down in 1996. By then, Hoffman had learned what he needed to know about software development and gained some experience in product management. He was ready to move on to the next item on his checklist: experience in building a team.

LEARNING BUSINESS MANAGEMENT

To learn how to manage a team and operate a business, Hoffman went to work at Fujitsu Software. He became head of product management and development of the Worlds-Away group at Fujitsu. The product was a different type of online community: a virtual world. Users who subscribed to the service and purchased the program could log on and interact with other people who were part of their "world." They created avatars—animated icons to represent themselves—and moved them around on their computer screens. They made the avatars "talk" by typing words into thought bubbles. The cartoonlike simulation may seem primitive by today's standards, but managing the Worlds-Away team gave Hoffman the knowledge he needed.

Fujitsu also gave Hoffman two new contacts who later became cofounders of LinkedIn. In answer to an advertisement for a programming engineer, Jean-Luc Vaillant had come from France to join the WorldsAway team. Like Hoffman, Vaillant was more interested in starting something new than working for a company that had been around since 1935.

The other budding entrepreneur Hoffman met through Fujitsu was Konstantin Guericke. Guericke was a German-born Stanford graduate, but Hoffman did not know him in college. He worked at a company that created virtual communities similar to Fujitsu's WorldsAway. He and Hoffman met when they each represented their companies at an avatar convention, and they became fast friends. Guericke was also interested in doing some kind of a computer start-up. The two got together every week and talked about different online sites— why some worked and why others failed. They brainstormed ideas for sites of their own. One would suggest a concept and the other would pick it apart. The casual weekly sessions were more than fun; they helped both men learn more about Internet businesses.

STEP 3: PLUNGING IN

While Hoffman was gaining knowledge and experience, the Internet was beginning to explode. When he graduated from Stanford in 1990, very few people had even heard of the Internet. Most businesses and many homes had computers, but they were used mainly for recording and storing information. They were not connected to one another outside company or school networks. But between 1993, when Hoffman graduated from Oxford University, and 1994, new technologies changed computer usage radically and rapidly. Hyperlinks were perfected that connected users in different countries, creating the World Wide Web.

Hoffman is seen here after a television interview in which he discussed social media and his book, *The Start-up of You.* Because of his business, tech, and relationship savvy, Hoffman is frequently asked to speak at conferences and for business media.

Netscape released a browser that made navigating the Web easy. Individuals as well as businesses were discovering that the Web was an exciting place. New sites were popping up all over. Internet usage in the spring of 1994 was growing at a rate of 2,300 percent every year!

Hoffman could not sit idly by, playing with avatars in a virtual world, while other people were starting and growing online businesses. He was concerned that the people with money might stop investing in new ideas. He felt he had the experience he needed, and he didn't want to wait. But creating his own Internet company would take time, energy, and focus. He couldn't continue in his job and give a new venture the attention it would need. So in 1997, he resigned his position at Fujitsu to launch his own company.

Hoffman knew that what he was doing was risky. Many start-ups failed. Those that succeeded often took years to actually make a profit. But Hoffman believed what he would write in his book, *The Start-up of You*, fifteen years later: "Take intelligent and bold risks to do something great." He did not make the move without considering the possibility of failure; he had a fallback position, a Plan Z. If the business totally flopped, he had a place he could live until he got on his feet again. When he came back from England, he had stayed with his grandparents until he landed the job at Apple. His father told him that if this enterprise folded, he could live with him while he looked for another opportunity. The fallback position took away some of the fear that always comes with risk.

Hoffman wasted no time putting together a team. A software start-up would need a variety of people: Web designers, product engineers, managers, financial officers, and others. As he had done before, he looked to his network. He recruited an engineer from Apple; Vaillant from Fujitsu; and a friend who had founded two online companies, *Gamepro* magazine and Infotainment World. Someone in his network introduced him to Allen Blue, a Stanford grad like himself. Blue's degrees were in drama and English, but he worked in the technical end of the theater industry, designing and building sets and scenery for San Francisco stage productions. He also created Web sites for a number of clients. Hoffman thought Blue could design the new company's product.

The product was a social networking service. Long before Myspace and Facebook made social networking popular, Hoffman saw the value of the Internet in connecting people. Millions were now logging on, and Hoffman thought he and his team could build an application that could help them find one another. They could design a technology that would match people with similar interests. Its most obvious use would be for dating, but people looking for roommates, tennis partners, or golf foursomes might

Friendster, the First Big Social Network

Networking online is as old as the Internet. But the early forms of connecting were very different from the social networking sites of today. The first cyber links between people were basically bulletin boards: people simply posted information and read what others wrote. For example, when

This photograph shows Friendster founder Jonathan Abrams in 2003, at the height of the company's popularity. The name "Friendster" was a takeoff on Napster, a site on which people shared music files.

Classmates.com started in 1995, a visitor could look up classmates but could not contact them directly through the Web site. After 2001, the Internet became more interactive.

In 2002, Jonathan Abrams founded Friendster to compete with Match.com. It connected people as far as four degrees, or steps, apart—friends of friends of friends of friends. Hoffman was one of the first investors in the company. Friendster was the first truly successful online social network. With an aggressive marketing campaign, it attracted more than three million members within the first few months. After just one year, Google tried to buy the company for $30 million, but Abrams turned the offer down.

That may have been a huge mistake, as Myspace, launched in 2003, overtook Friendster in popularity and then Facebook eclipsed both. As membership dropped, the company turned to networkers overseas. In 2009, Friendster was purchased by MOL Global, Asia's largest Internet provider. In 2011, the company discontinued social networking entirely and became a social gaming site.

also link up. At first Hoffman called it Relationship.com, but he quickly changed the name to SocialNet.

LEARNING FROM MISTAKES

SocialNet was not the first social networking site. In 1995, Match.com had appeared on the Internet. Hoffman thought he could produce something similar but better. He concentrated on designing a superior matching program. He had some difficulty obtaining financing but was eventually able to sell his idea to some venture capitalists, and he had $1.7 million to start up.

Hoffman found that creating the product was easy, but marketing it was a lot harder. His plan was to partner with some print media. He would place ads in newspapers and magazines, people would read about the site, and they would go online to try it. But the plan did not work; ads in one Arizona paper generated only two customers in the first month.

Hoffman knew he had to change the distribution strategy. How could he get his matching site in front of millions of people? Millions of people do not read the same newspapers and magazines. He realized too late that the only way a product or service can "go viral"—spread quickly on the Internet, like a virus—is to have the mechanism for spreading it built into the way it works. Social-Net's marketing plan was "old school"; it presumed people looking for other people turned first to printed classified ads. He needed to change the Web site to attract people so that they would start their searches on the site.

But members of the company's board thought a television advertising campaign would bring more customers. Hoffman could not convince them that his plan would be better. They insisted on a distribution strategy Hoffman was convinced would not be successful. The board sold SocialNet later, in 2001, but Hoffman was ready to leave at the end of 1999. It was time, he knew, to pivot to a new plan.

CHAPTER 3

Plan B: PayPal

When Hoffman knew SocialNet would not be the big success he had hoped, he did not give up. He looked at the venture as a learning experience and was determined to try again with another business idea. But what? He was sold on the concept of social networking because he believed that relationships were really important. He called on someone in his personal network to discuss what he might do next.

That someone was Peter Thiel, the friend he had met in a philosophy class at Stanford more than ten years earlier. Thiel had cofounded his own company shortly after Hoffman launched SocialNet. Hoffman was actually helping him, providing advice and serving on the founding board. The company was a start-up called PayPal.

THE COMPANY

PayPal began in 1998, when Thiel was invited to give a lecture at his alma mater, Stanford University. An attendee at

Peter Thiel (*left*) and Elon Musk display PayPal's logo on a computer screen. Thiel's company, Confinity, merged with Musk's company, X.com, and the new company became PayPal.

that lecture, Max Levchin, talked to Thiel about a business idea. Levchin was a programming engineer and Thiel was a financial trader; together, they made a team that was perfect for creating an online financial product. Within weeks of their first meeting, they launched a company called Fieldlink.

Fieldlink's product was a digital wallet, a means of storing financial information electronically. At that time, the Palm Pilot was the latest electronic gadget. The forerunner of smartphones, it was the first device that

The Palm Pilot was one of the first PDAs—personal digital assistants. A handheld device advertised as a one-touch organizer, it stored addresses, appointments, to-do items, and memos.

enabled people to carry large amounts of information in the palms of their hands. But no one put their bank account data into their Palm Pilots for fear that others could access their financial information. Thiel and Levchin developed an encryption platform—a way to encode information— for Palm Pilots and similar devices. Now users could feel safe having their bank accounts at their fingertips. Fieldlink was more secure than carrying actual cash because the money was safe in the bank and only the owner of the electronic device could move it.

Thiel and Levchin further developed their product so that people with Palm Pilots could send and receive cash to and from one another. They changed the name of the company to Confinity, combining the idea of confidence in the security of the exchange with the notion of infinite possibilities. When they found a way to transfer money through e-mail instead of with Palm Pilots, they called the online service PayPal. When bidders on the online auction site eBay discovered PayPal, many began using it for their eBay purchases. The one-year-old company was just beginning to take off when Hoffman came to talk with Thiel about his own plans.

THE PIVOT

Hoffman told Thiel he was going to leave the company he founded and create another start-up. In his two years at SocialNet, he had learned a lot—about himself, about the Internet, and about building a business. He thought he was now in a better position to go out on his own and succeed. But his friend told him to wait. PayPal, he said, was ready to explode; it could be dynamite. He could use more help than Hoffman was supplying by just being on the board. Thiel asked him to come to work with him full-time. He would not need to commit to a long time . . . probably no more than six months.

Hoffman considered his options. He fully intended to launch a new company, but it would take him a while to get a start-up going. In the meantime, he would need a paying job. He could either find a short-term position somewhere in the tech field or he could accept Thiel's offer. He thought long and hard about the choices and decided to go with PayPal. He called it "pivoting to a breakout opportunity." Pivoting meant changing direction, turning from Plan A to Plan B.

Hoffman resigned from SocialNet in January 2000 and began his new assignment the very next day. His title at PayPal was executive vice president; he was in charge of external relations. That meant he dealt with everything and everybody outside the company that made the whole operation work: banks, government regulators, credit card companies, and partnering businesses. Thiel told the *New York Times* that Hoffman was PayPal's "firefighter in chief." And, he said, "there were many, many fires."

PUTTING OUT FIRES

The challenges turned out to be far more and much greater than either Thiel or Hoffman had imagined. Thiel later told *Bloomberg* the situation was like being in a tiny rowboat that was about to go over a giant waterfall: everyone was rowing with all their might to keep the company afloat.

The first set of challenges came from growing pains. As more and more eBay customers began using PayPal, the company had to change the way it operated. It dropped the Palm Pilot services and concentrated on Internet money transfers. That meant developing relationships with credit card companies and other financial institutions, as well as businesses that bought and sold online. It meant creating new systems and procedures. All of that had to be done quickly because the company was growing at a phenomenal rate. In January, Hoffman's first month on the job, PayPal had one hundred thousand accounts. By March, that number had risen to one million.

In March, the company grew in another way: it merged with another company. New personnel came on board. A second office was opened, outside of Silicon Valley, in Nebraska. PayPal's success attracted hackers, and the company lost millions of dollars because of fraud. As an example of the size of some of the difficulties, in a single month PayPal had zero income and $12 million in outgo.

Hoffman was up to the challenges. What made him a great asset to PayPal was the high value he placed on relationships. When he met people, he tried to see situations from their perspectives. He usually thought about how he could help them, not about what they could do for him. So when someone was unhappy with PayPal, Hoffman was the man who got the assignment of patching things up. Moreover, he generally succeeded. He spent lots of time building relationships with the companies that worked with PayPal. He met regularly with people in the banking, regulatory, and Internet industries. His six-month stint stretched to almost three years.

THE BIGGEST FIRE

The most serious threat to PayPal came from Visa and MasterCard. Executives at these credit card companies did not understand how the online money transfers worked. Online buyers and sellers went through PayPal to move their funds into or out of their credit card accounts because they could not access those accounts directly. The credit card companies were used to paper transactions, and they did not trust electronic transfers; they weren't sure they would get their money. Every time a problem came up, they became more suspicious of the start-up that did business in such a new way. Unfortunately, problems did arise. Any new venture has bugs that have to be worked out, and PayPal was no different. The problems were small, but the big companies were afraid they might become major. At one point, Visa was going to stop doing business with the new company. That would have been the death of PayPal.

Thiel and the other cofounders could not trust the Visa account to anyone but Hoffman. When Hoffman met with Visa's executives, his objective was to convince Visa to continue working with PayPal for at least a year; that was all the time he needed. By then, he was sure, the glitches would be corrected and Visa would be confident and happy with the arrangement. What the Visa people wanted was to know that PayPal did not have any problems that threatened them.

Hoffman listened to Visa's executives and looked at the issue from their point of view. They were worried about the high number of chargebacks that were coming from PayPal users. Hoffman knew that Visa was a huge corporation that did things slowly and methodically. People at Visa studied issues thoroughly before making decisions. Hoffman worked out a compromise that suited both companies: Visa would conduct a series of studies to find out if the chargebacks were really a problem, and, while the studies were underway, PayPal could keep the Visa

The PayPal logo was added to the sign in front of eBay's headquarters in San Jose, California, after the online auction site purchased PayPal.

account. Reid Hoffman scored a major win that kept his company alive and also kept revenue coming into Visa.

BIG SUCCESS

Hoffman's ability to build relationships did more than keep the company alive; it helped it thrive. More and more, eBay users were discovering the convenience and speed of PayPal. The team decided to take PayPal public. That meant that instead of the team owning the company, they would let other people buy shares in it; it would change from being privately owned to being publicly owned. They would use the money the people paid for the shares to grow the company even more. The initial public offering (IPO) was made on February 15, 2002. The com-pany offered, or put up for sale, 5.4 million shares at $13 per share. By the time the stock market closed that day, each share was

The PayPal Mafia—the Founders and Early Employees

Executive	Role at PayPal	Later Ventures
Botha, Roelof	CFO	Sequoia Capital, managing partner
Chen, Steve	Engineer	YouTube, cofounder
Hoffman, Reid	Executive VP	• LinkedIn, cofounder and executive chairman • Greylock, partner
Hurley, Chad	Designer	YouTube, cofounder
Karim, Jawed	Engineer	YouTube, cofounder
Levchin, Max	Cofounder, CTO	Slide, founder
McClure, Dave	Director of marketing	• 500 Start-ups, founding partner • Kiva, adviser
Musk, Elon	Cofounder, director	• SpaceX, founder and CEO • Tesla, cofounder and CEO
Rabols, Keith	Executive VP, business development	• Square, COO • YouTube, investor • Geni, investor • LinkedIn, investor • Yelp, investor
Sachs, David	COO	• Yammer, cofounder and CEO • Geni, chairman
Shah, Premal	Product manager	Kiva, president
Simmons, Russel	Engineer	Yelp, cofounder
Stoppelman, Jeremy	VP, engineering	Yelp, cofounder and CEO
Thiel, Peter	Cofounder, CEO	• Clarium Capital, president • Facebook, board director • Founders Fund, managing partner

worth over $20 and PayPal had netted more than $61 million.

After three years of "scratching and clawing" to survive, as one PayPal employee put it, the company finally appeared to be on the path to success. Yet another threat loomed large, this time from eBay. Many buyers and sellers on the online auction site were using PayPal, but eBay had its own payment system, and it wanted people to use that system. EBay was PayPal's biggest customer, but it was also its strongest competitor. The feud went on for months, and PayPal was winning.

EBay decided it was easier to buy the competition than beat it. Four times eBay made offers, and Hoffman was one of the chief negotiators. EBay had an edge: more than half of PayPal's profits came from transferring money on eBay sales, and PayPal could not afford to lose that business. On the fifth round of discussions an agreement was reached: eBay bought PayPal for $1.5 billion. All of PayPal's executives owned shares in the company and they all made money when it was sold . . . lots of money. Executive Vice President Reid Hoffman became a multimillionaire.

"PAYPAL MAFIA"

None of the PayPal employees remained at eBay very long. They went their separate ways, but many of them stayed connected to one another. They had been through a lot together; the PayPal experience had been a roller coaster of hard-fought battles, thrilling victories, and close calls. They had learned together, lost together, and won big together. They had a special kind of camaraderie.

They began calling themselves the "PayPal Mafia." Other people started using the name after a 2007 article appeared in *Fortune* magazine titled "Meet the PayPal Mafia." For the magazine, thirteen ex-PayPal executives met at Tosca Café, a posh San Francisco bar. Dressed in 1920s-style gangster attire and attempting to look menacing, they posed for a group picture. They acknowledged Peter Thiel as the don, the godfather, or leader of the group.

In many ways, the men were alike. *Fortune* called them "hyperintelligent and superconnected." Thiel and Levchin had hired people who were much like themselves. They had wanted people who were college graduates, good at math, able to speak more than one language, liked to read, and were competitive—and they got them. Most had been recruited either from Stanford—Thiel's school—or the University of Illinois—Levchin's alma mater. The guys of the PayPal Mafia were not

PayPal cofounder Max Levchin (*right*) talks to a *Bloomberg Businessweek* writer. Printed on his shirt is "Slide," the name of the Internet company Levchin started when he left PayPal.

business majors, preppies, or athletes; they were ambitious young men who would rather work than play.

Although they were alike in the ways they thought and acted, they had different strengths. They were engineers, designers, marketers, managers, and financial people. Some were idea men, others were detail oriented, and still others were people persons. Together, they made a formidable team.

They all had ideas, drive, and energy, and after PayPal was sold, they all had money. They used the money they made from PayPal to invest in different companies, begin their own investment firms, and donate to worthwhile charities. Others who made money from successful start-ups also used their wealth for new ventures, but no other single group created as many profitable and innovative enterprises as the PayPal Mafia. The few men in that group were instrumental in founding, developing, or funding YouTube, Zynga, Facebook, Flickr, Mozilla, LinkedIn, Groupon, Tesla Motors, and scores of other very popular businesses.

Although they used their tremendous fortunes to make more money, some of them spent a little of the bonanza on creature comforts. After all, they had been through some lean times at PayPal. Thiel spent well over $150,000 on a Ferrari. Hoffman thought about buying an Audi at about half what his friend paid for his vehicle, but he hesitated. He thought: if this was all the money he had, would he rather spend it on a fancy car or on something that might change the world? He did not need to think hard; his long-standing value—everyone should make an impact for good—made the decision easy. He put some of his money into Nanosolar, an early solar panel company. Encouraging the use of solar energy seemed a way to make a positive impact. His car was pretty old, so he bought an Acura for considerably less than either the Ferrari or the Audi.

But what would he do with the bulk of his wealth? What about his time—what should he pour his energies into? He was only thirty-five years old—what would he do with the rest of his life?

CHAPTER 4

New Plan A: LinkedIn

Hoffman wasn't sure what he wanted to do after Pay-Pal. He thought he might take a year or so away from any job. Life had been pretty hectic; maybe just relaxing and traveling would be good. He'd start with a two-week vacation in Australia. That would give him an opportunity away from the hustle and bustle of Silicon Valley to think and plan. But he couldn't get Silicon Valley and his dream of a start-up out of his mind. Internet business was still young and entrepreneurs had barely begun to tap its possibilities. Dozens of people must be working on ideas for new online companies, and they could beat him to the money if he waited. He knew lots of people who might work with him, even beyond his Pay-Pal friends. But he needed to talk with them before they were too busy with dreams of their own. No, he decided, now was not the time for a yearlong vacation. Now was the time to create and launch a brand new enterprise.

"DOT-COM WINTER"

Not many people agreed with Hoffman. Many thought the consumer Internet—the system of buying everyday products online—was dead. Hoffman described the mood among entrepreneurs as "dot-com winter." At the end of 2002, investors and businesspeople alike were still reeling from the effects of what has become known as the dot-com bust—the bursting of a giant economic bubble.

The bubble had begun in the mid-1990s, after Mosaic and Netscape browsers opened the World Wide Web to the general public. After Amazon created a splash with its cyber bookstore, companies sprang up offering everything from pet food to designer clothes. The idea of selling goods and services through computers was new and exciting and seemed to be the wave of the future. Everyone with any technical ability wanted to get in on the action. They wanted to get in quickly and corner their particular markets before others edged them out. Investors were also eager to be part of what looked like a gold mine. Low interest rates in 1998 and 1999 encouraged investment and helped the bubble expand.

The rush to be at the forefront of the new economy caused many to abandon traditional financial practices. Instead of concentrating on making profits, their strategy was to do whatever it took to attract lots of customers— even if it meant losing money. The thinking was: get big

At the New York Stock Exchange, traders hurry to make their sales or purchases before the exchange closes for the day. The dot-com crash occurred from about March 2000 to October 2002.

fast, and then make money. So in the beginning, Internet companies offered free shipping, spent huge amounts on advertising, and even gave products away. They operated in the red—spending far more than they took in. They spent millions hoping to eventually make billions. In the excitement, the prices of their stocks soared, based not on actual value, but on what the businesses expected to make. Before long, the Internet was flooded with companies, all competing for the same customers. The bubble was getting bigger and thinner.

In 2000, the bubble burst. It did not pop like a balloon; it deflated over the course of several months and the next year. The value of the stocks of Internet companies plummeted. Investors pulled their money out. Nearly all lost much of their money, and many went completely broke. Successes like PayPal were the exception. The dot-com bust plunged the entire country into an economic recession. In October 2002, when Hoffman was deciding where to go next, hardly anyone was trying to start an online business. Tech entrepreneurs were discouraged, investors had been burned, and the public was skeptical.

But Hoffman thought those were the perfect conditions for a tech start-up. If others were leery of Internet business, their fear left plenty of room for him. If investors did not want to risk their funds, he would bankroll his start-up himself; he had money from his PayPal shares.

Web 1.0, 2.0, and 3.0

The Internet and the Web are two different things. The Internet, or Net, is a network that connects computers to one another. A computer can communicate with any other computer that is connected to the Internet. The Web is a set of documents that are on the Internet. In other words, the Net is a collection of computers and

Reid Hoffman was one of the speakers at the 2011 Web 2.0 Expo, a conference presenting the latest technologies for Web users.

the Web is a collection of pieces of information. The Net holds the Web.

Since the Web was introduced in the 1990s, the way its information is presented and accessed has evolved. In its first form, now called Web 1.0, information was posted and all users could do was read it. Nothing on a page could be changed until a Webmaster updated it. After the dot-com bust, Web 2.0 emerged. Web 2.0 is sometimes called the "social Web." It is interactive; users can present and change information (for example, review products, write and comment on blogs, make and post YouTube videos). They can use links and tags to connect pieces of information. And they can upload and download information not only on computers, but also on cell phones, electronic pads, and other devices.

Web 3.0 cannot be far off. It will access information not by Web site (1.0) or keyword (2.0), but by any piece of data. Programmers predict the new generation of the Web will not simply recognize information, but understand it. It will allow users to find, share, and combine the exact information they want and filter out what they do not need. Best of all, it will do it at record speeds.

If the public was uncertain, he would simply produce a product that people couldn't live without.

THE IDEA

What would that product be? Hoffman had lots of ideas. Some might have been a little unusual; he thought about time capsules that let people store their pictures and other memories online and retrieve them later. Other ideas seemed more practical. The one he kept coming back to was a little like SocialNet: some kind of service that would connect people. But he was not thinking of a dating site; he was interested in workplace connections.

While at PayPal, Hoffman realized that the world of work was changing. In his father's generation, people climbed career ladders, beginning with little knowledge or skills and advancing in a series of steps to higher-paying positions. They usually stayed at one company, or at least in one field, all of their professional lives. Once a person landed that first, entry-level job, the rest was often fairly smooth sailing. But in the twenty-first century, the ladder was harder to climb. More people were competing for the same spots, so moving up was not automatic. Companies no longer trained their employees for the next rung because they could easily hire a new person who already had the skills for the job. Instead of retiring after thirty years in one company, people changed jobs after a few years or a few months. Creative people were inventing products and technologies that called for new skills and different ways of thinking and operating.

One clear way the business world had changed, as Hoffman saw it, was that doing well depended less on the company than on the worker. In the past, the company set the pay and determined how employees advanced. In the highly mobile computer age, however, people could negotiate their salaries and move to better positions in different firms. People, not businesses, seemed to have the upper hand. It seemed that each individual was like his or her own company and people were thinking like CEOs of their own careers. They could take charge of their own professional identities, set their own employment goals, and manage their own careers.

Hoffman was convinced that the new way to work centered on networking. The way to find information, opportunities, and resources in any job or career is to connect with people. Hoffman had gotten his jobs at Apple, Fujitsu, and PayPal by networking. He was able to put out the fires at PayPal because he had built relationships with people in the computer, finance, and regulatory industries. In the workplace of the future, where people serious about moving up in their careers needed to direct their own lives, meeting and contacting the right people would be critical. What if he built a product that helped professionals to network? That is something that would make a great impact for good in the world of work.

REFINING THE IDEA

Social networking was not a new concept. The early forms were based on the theory of six degrees of separation. Sociologists had long toyed with the thought that every human being could be connected with any other human being through chains of six people. Person A knows Person B, who knows Person C, and so on down to Person F. The idea is that if all the right matchups could be found, no two people would be more than six degrees—or five people—apart. In theory, then, building networks that show who is linked to whom and how closely would make it easier for people to find and make the connections they want.

The more Hoffman thought about a network for professionals, the more sense it made. In the business world, opportunities were often governed not by what a person knew, but whom. Getting to know the right people sometimes required a couple steps: a friend knew a friend. An online product would have to work in much the same way as effective networking did in the real world—

people would introduce their first-degree friends to each other, and that would generate new relationship chains. Hoffman was convinced it could be done.

Linking people professionally was a natural fit for Hoffman. He had always believed in the importance of relationships. He and Konstantin Guericke had talked about a business network back during his days at Fujitsu, when they were both building virtual worlds. Guericke had bought the domain name People Map. He was going to create a Web site that combined a homepage for professionals, an online address book, and some way to let users meet new people. They discussed the idea, but they didn't have the resources to develop it at that time. Hoffman began SocialNet instead, a much simpler site. But five years later, itching to do a start-up, he still thought a professional network was his best bet.

Hoffman's network would not be the first social media site. Six Degrees had been launched in 1997 and had fallen victim to the dot-com bust in 2001. Others had begun after the bust: Plaxo, Ecademy, VisiblePath, Spoke, and tribe. Ryze, the first online link-up focused on businesses, already had forty thousand members. Friendster, a popular social network in which Hoffman had invested, could easily add a business feature. The market was beginning to get crowded. If Hoffman was going to get in, he needed to act fast.

Konstantin Guericke, one of LinkedIn's cofounders and its marketing director, explains how the company's concept of connecting friends of friends works.

THE START

In December 2002, barely two months after eBay bought PayPal, Hoffman gathered four of his friends in his tiny apartment. They were men in his personal and business networks, people he had worked with and knew well. Three of the four were graduates of Stanford, like himself, although they did not know one another in school. Like Hoffman, they were all young, talented, highly educated go-getters. All had experience in Internet start-ups.

One of the men was Guericke, who shared Hoffman's enthusiasm for business networking. A successful marketer, he had helped over a dozen executives start new businesses. Another was Eric Ly, who had worked for the computer giants IBM and Sun Microsystems before beginning two start-ups of his own. Alan Blue was a creative Web designer who had worked with Hoffman at SocialNet, Hoffman's first

As Hoffman poses for a picture at LinkedIn's headquarters, he demonstrates that the typical business dress of many Internet CEOs is not a three-piece suit but shorts and a comfortable shirt.

attempt at a start-up. The lone non-Stanford grad, Jean-Luc Vaillant, was an engineering genius who had also worked with Hoffman at SocialNet as well as at Fujitsu on the WorldsAway project.

For months, these five men had talked about doing a start-up together. They had tossed ideas back and forth and settled on an Internet site that would connect professionals to one another. They had toyed with a prototype—a test model. They worked on the project as a hobby on the weekends. But as more networks popped up on his computer screen, Hoffman grew antsy. Those companies were already online and his team was still talking, still just dabbling. That is why he called the team together in December.

The meeting was productive; all five men were in. They all had good jobs, but that day they decided to quit their secure positions, walk away from guaranteed incomes, and devote their time to an untried, unproven dream.

What would they call it? They needed a domain name—a title that would catch people's attention, give them an idea of what the site was about, and be easy to remember. Guericke had sold the People Map name, so that was out. Everyone liked Well Connected, but it was already taken. They tried In, but it was not available either. Domain names were assigned by a private company, and people often bought them, as Guericke had, in case they would use them later or to resell them at a higher price. The best ones could be expensive, and the team had decided not to

Unauthorized Links

In June 2012, a cyber sleuth in Norway detected that someone had gotten into LinkedIn's Web site (and others' sites) and uploaded the passwords of nearly 6.5 million LinkedIn members. The hacker published the passwords on a Russian site, asking fellow hackers for help in decoding the stolen passwords. It was every Internet user's worst nightmare: not merely one criminal in a far-away country, but anyone with a computer had access to their account. Anyone could learn where they worked, who they worked with, what appointments they had and when, and any number of other pieces of personal information. They could use that data to break into their other online accounts.

LinkedIn took immediate action. The company determined that the encryption, or coding, of some of the passwords had indeed been cracked, enabling unauthorized people to get into accounts. Those accounts were disabled and their owners were walked through the process of establishing new passwords. Security was restored, but confidence was shaken. How easily could it happen again?

The answer was a frightening "very easily." LinkedIn had been using an old method of hashing, or encrypting members' usernames and pass-words. For about ten years, other companies had been both hashing and salting—adding another layer of scrambling to the process of disguising people's online identities. LinkedIn had relied on an outdated, inadequate method, and its members were not protected. Within days of the breach, LinkedIn had newer, more modern security measures in place. The company will need to continue to create even more sophisticated tools to keep ahead of the ever-present hackers.

pay more than $5,000 for a name. The men finally settled on "LinkedIn." No one was thrilled with the "linked" part, but they all liked "in." So they put a blue square around "in" to make it stand out. Then they prepared to launch.

CINCO DE LINKEDIN

Within five months, they were ready to go live. They were careful to keep their work secret. Their plan was to start up, engage a good number of people, find out what would interest and help them, and build the site around those needs. They weren't sure everything would work properly at the beginning, and it could take some time to perfect the site. So they wanted a stealth launch.

But they would need enough people to make the site worth coming to. Hoffman's target was a million because he was always interested in a big scale. What would be the point of a network unless it had people to connect with? Hoffman reached into his own network to add six more people to his founding team. Four had worked at Social-Net (David Eves, Ian McNish, Chris Saccheri, and Yan Pujante), one at Apple (Stephen Beitzel), and one at PayPal (Lee Hower). Together with the five who had first met in Hoffman's front room, they would form the core of the company. These eleven would then encourage the people in their networks to become part of the new venture. They, in turn, would invite people they knew, and the company would grow.

When everything was ready, Jean-Luc Vaillant, vice president of engineering, sent e-mails to each of the founding members. The subject line read, "Jean-Luc Vaillant invites you to connect." The message was, "We're good, invite each other now." The date was May 5—in Spanish, "Cinco de Mayo," a day many in Mexico celebrate. It commemorates the unlikely victory of a small Mexican force over a large French army in 1862. Hoffman and his team dubbed the date Cinco de LinkedIn. On that day in 2003, not far from San Francisco, another Frenchman led a tiny army of eleven entrepreneurs onto an Internet battlefield against a growing number of competitors.

CHAPTER 5

Permanent Beta: Growing LinkedIn

Although several networking sites were already in the field, LinkedIn was decidedly different. It would be another year before the term "social media" would be coined, but the other sites were definitely social. Some of the more popular ones focused on dating. The ones that presented themselves as catering to businesspeople were little more than digital address books. A few tried to appeal to people looking for professional contacts as well as those wanting to find friends. Hoffman was adamant that people coming to his site would know it was not about personal relationships or having fun; it was about business.

A NEW KIND OF COMPANY

The LinkedIn team worked hard on distinguishing its product from all the others. One way the team separated the new company from its competitors was to launch it without photos. This would communicate visually

The "3rd" located after Hoffman's name on his LinkedIn (www.linkedin.com) profile page indicates that he is a third-degree contact to the member who accessed this page. The page gives the names of the other contacts.

Reid Hoffman | L

E_SEARCH&   ↻   Q▾ lin|

panies   More

o or Location Business Port

at LinkedIn ☐
uestbridge   .

that the site would not promote social contacts, but would foster workplace connections. Professionals would not visit LinkedIn to merely look around in their spare time; they would come deliberately to search for someone or something specific that would help them in their jobs.

Most of the business networking sites that were on the Web in early 2003 were fairly simple. Anyone could log on, search, and connect with someone. It was easy to amass a large group of contacts. But Hoffman felt there was a big difference between contacts and relationships: contacts are names on a list; relationships are people you know and talk with. In the real world of shops and offices, people do not do business with names on a list. They do not offer jobs to people they do not know. They ask their friends to introduce them to the ones they want to work with. They get referrals from people they know and trust. LinkedIn connected people through introductions.

Not everyone could participate; they had to be invited. The original eleven members invited their friends to join. New members invited their friends. Once people were members, they could look around the site and see who else was a part. But they couldn't just contact another member. They had to contact one of their friends—someone who had invited them or who they had invited—and ask that person to introduce them to the one they wanted to meet. Members were careful about who they connected with whom because they had some level of relationship with both parties.

They were also careful about their own identities. The other social media were very public; anyone who clicked on a name could see everything that person was willing to share about himself or herself. And some people shared a lot of frivolous information. LinkedIn, by contrast, was very private. Profiles had to be strictly professional, with no personal details.

This new way of networking not only made LinkedIn feel more professional than the other business sites, but it also kept it from one of the big problems the other companies had. They had become "spammy." That is, advertisers and individuals were taking advantage of readily available lists of names and e-mail addresses and flooding people with messages promoting their products. Anyone could send a message to anyone else, and it seemed that everyone did. But they couldn't do that on LinkedIn. Hoffman was pleased with his product. He felt it truly could make the world a better place.

PERMANENT BETA

But he didn't have a solid business plan, a blueprint for where the company was going and how it would get there. That was by design. Hoffman believed a business should always be in what he called "permanent beta." "Beta" is the term software developers use for the final phase of testing their products before they are released to the general public. In the beta phase, the engineers work out the bugs, adapt to conditions they didn't expect, and make the product better. Hoffman thought every company should always be in beta mode— continually evolving, adjusting, and improving.

The way some Web sites try to keep up with what their customers want is to ask users to fill out online surveys. Hoffman, however, sincerely believed what he used for the tagline, or motto, for LinkedIn: relationships matter. He did not want electronic feedback from impersonal surveys; he wanted to hear from actual customers—firsthand, out loud, and face-to-face. If someone had a problem with his service, he wanted to be able to ask that person questions so that he could find out exactly what needed to be fixed. To get that information, Hoffman and some of the other team members had lunch regularly with people who were using LinkedIn. Over salad or hamburgers, in a very natural and relaxed way, these customers shared their experiences, and the team learned what their clients liked and disliked about the site. In this way, by starting his company with the idea of being in permanent beta, Hoffman built a business that delivered what its users wanted.

SPREADING THE WORD

Because LinkedIn's business plan was evolving, Hoffman did not want publicity at the start. He knew it would be months before the Web site was functioning smoothly, and he did not want to promote it until its operation was a little more solid. He did, however, hope that the stealth launch would create a little bit of excitement about the site. But he was not pleased with the small stir it created. Most of the bloggers, the Internet "journalists" who reported what was new in the online world, did not like the new company. They didn't like the idea of separating people's personal and professional lives. They were not happy with all the privacy controls. It looked like a social site that wasn't very social. The popular networking sites of the time were much more attractive and fun, and the bloggers saw no need for another one, especially one that seemed so dull. They wrote that LinkedIn was a poor company and it would never work.

One blogger, however, was positive, and he had a big following. Rafe Needleman was the editor of the online magazine *Redherring.com.* He wrote an e-mail and Web column for that magazine called "Catch of the Day" that was read by more than one hundred thousand people. The column reviewed new Internet companies the editor considered likely to be successful. When he selected LinkedIn as the Catch of the Day, a few more people began looking at the site.

The best publicity did not come from bloggers; it came from people who actually used the product. The first few members had enlarged their networks so that at the end of the first month, May 2003, 4,500 people were using the site. Before long, some of them had found new jobs through their contacts at LinkedIn. Established executives had expanded their businesses and increased their profits because of the connections they made on LinkedIn. The company had success stories it could tell, and tell them it did. The stories showed the value of the networking site and let people see how it worked. More people joined. By the time LinkedIn was a year old, it boasted more than half a million members.

Konstantin Guericke stands with Hoffman at LinkedIn's office in 2005, two years after the company's launch. At that time, LinkedIn had four million members. It would not become profitable for another year.

ATTRACTING INVESTORS

The members paid nothing to join. The team had ideas for making the business pay for itself in time, but at the beginning all the services were free. At the same time, the site cost money to run. During the development phase and for the first five months of operation, Hoffman paid the bills. But his PayPal money would eventually run out. Entrepreneurs with start-ups typically look for investors to put cash into their companies until the businesses begin to make a profit. Hoffman, however, did not need to look for an investor; an investor found him.

The venture capitalist firm Sequoia Capital was searching for up-and-coming companies that looked like they might become big. Businesses as well as individuals could join the growing networks at LinkedIn, and one of Sequoia's partners signed his company up. He used the services, and he liked them. The company's very clear and very narrow focus on business referrals got his attention. He was impressed with the stories people on the Web site told of how LinkedIn had helped them. The partner asked Hoffman if he would let Sequoia invest in his start-up. So in October 2003, when LinkedIn was barely five months old, Sequoia Capital opened the first round of investment in the fledgling company, called series A funding, with $4.7 million.

Other investment firms also noticed LinkedIn. They, too, were impressed with the company's unique features and the way it was growing. They thought it had the potential to overtake Ryze, then the biggest business network on the Internet. A year after LinkedIn received its first investment funds, in October 2004, Greylock led series B financing with $10 million. Others jumped in with money for what they saw as a great opportunity, including Hoffman's friend Peter Thiel.

ADDING FEATURES

When companies invest millions of dollars into a business, they are betting that the business will make much more. Hoffman's team concentrated on making LinkedIn profitable. In 2005 it launched three revenue streams—three ways money would flow into the company. The first was through job listings. The job listings entity was different from the traditional job board, which was simply a bulletin board of openings. On the LinkedIn feature, companies posted available jobs and invited their contacts to refer people they knew. Individual members could find positions that interested them and see if anyone in their network was connected with the companies that were hiring. The search was free to individual members, and companies paid $95 to post a job opening for thirty days. The cost was considerably more than the $9.95 Ryze charged its members for its gold-level job search feature. But LinkedIn billed companies, not individuals, and the companies were getting good value for the fee. They didn't have to pay to advertise anywhere else.

The second revenue stream was subscriptions, mostly for job recruiters. Members paid a monthly or yearly subscription fee and received premium services. A premium service is an upgrade, a feature that is available only to subscribers. Subscriptions were introduced in August 2005 at costs ranging from $60 to $2,000 per year, depending on which services were included in the member's premium account.

The third revenue stream was advertising. For some time, the team resisted allowing advertising on the site,

Two employees work in LinkedIn's main office in Mountain View, California. In 2012, the company employed worldwide more than 2,861 people full-time.

wanting to keep the look clean and professional. But Hoffman recognized that advertising certain products made sense on a business site and his team could build some unique ways of advertising them.

As the revenue streams began to take hold, new features appeared on the LinkedIn site in rapid succession: profile pictures, a newsfeed that kept members updated on their contacts, a mobile Web site, networking groups, a corporate blog, and a multitude of premium services. Every single feature supported LinkedIn's original mission, its purpose as a company: connecting the world's professionals to make them more productive and successful.

LinkedIn's Steady and Rapid Growth

Date	Number of Members
May 31, 2003	4,500
End of 2003	81,000
April 2004	0.5 million
August 2004	1 million
February 2005	2 million
June 2005	3 million
End of 2005	4 million
End of 2006	8 million
April 2007	10 million
September 2007	14 million
End of 2008	33 million
October 2009	50 million
February 2010	60 million
June 2010	70 million
March 2011	100 million
November 2011	135 million

GROWTH AND CHALLENGES

A year after LinkedIn began offering premium paid subscription services, in March 2006, the company began to make profits. With the profits came more investment. In 2007 and 2008, LinkedIn received $88.5 million from several venture capitalists. It continued developing features, and membership figures soared. LinkedIn partnered with media outlets—the *New York Times*, CNBC, and *Businessweek*—to provide news content for their Web sites tailored to LinkedIn members' profiles. It expanded to new countries. Hoffman was operating according to his three most important values: he was making an impact for good through relationships on a massive scale.

But success, especially rapid success, sometimes brings challenges. Just after the company became profitable, in the summer of 2006, Hoffman saw some potential problems on the horizon. The products division of the company was not evolving as quickly as the market, developing new applications for new demands. He needed to put someone in charge of the products team who would run the division in permanent beta mode. Hoffman made a decision: he knew software development, so he would manage the products team and hire someone else to replace him as chief executive officer (CEO).

Hoffman found his replacement through LinkedIn. He hired Dan Nye, an executive manager at Advent Software, a global computer company. During Nye's two years as LinkedIn's CEO, membership nearly quadrupled—from nine million to thirty-five million—and sales shot up 900 percent. To accommodate the explosive growth, the company added employees.

A member can access LinkedIn on a computer, a phone, a tablet, or other electronic device, making the services available just about anywhere.

But then a shake-up came. Reid Hoffman did not really enjoy running the day-to-day operations of the products team. He preferred managing people and inspiring vision. So he looked for someone else to serve as vice president of product management. When he found that person, Deep Nishar, Hoffman resumed his position as the company's CEO and Nye left. At about the same time, Hoffman tightened his company's operations, which meant laying off thirty-six people. The years 2008 and 2009 were turbulent but exciting for LinkedIn. The economic recession that hit the country actually boosted activity on LinkedIn's Web site. Out-of-work people were signing up to look for jobs, and companies that were hiring were happy to have the various services of LinkedIn screen applicants for them. Membership and profits continued to grow.

LinkedIn's Biggest Shareholders Prior to Its IPO

Shareholder	Number of Shares	Percent Ownership
Reid Hoffman and wife, Michelle Yee	19.1 million	21.4
Sequoia Capital	16.8 million	18.9
Greylock Partners	14.0 million	15.8
Bessemer Venture	4.6 million	5.1
Jeffrey Weiner, CEO	3.8 million	4.1
Steven Sordello, CFO	1.0 million	1.1
Deep Nishar, VP, Product	1.0 million	1.1

Source: Ben Parr, "LinkedIn's IPO: An Overview," Mashable Business, retrieved July 23, 2011 (http://mashable.com/2011/01/28/linkedins-ipo-an-overview).

GOING PUBLIC

By the middle of May 2011, LinkedIn was ready for its next big move: an IPO. Hoffman would take his start-up public, offering shares to others, and bringing an infusion of cash that would permit it to continue evolving to meet the ever-changing needs of the marketplace. By that time, Hoffman had hired a new CEO, Jeffrey Weiner, and had assumed for himself the position of chairman of the company.

In the official papers that LinkedIn filed for the IPO, Hoffman planned to sell 7,840,000 shares of stock, which accounted for 8 percent of the value of the company. He priced them at between $32 and $35 per share. After deducting fees and other expenses, he expected the sale would net the company $175 million. If he could get his asking price, the value of the company would be about $3 billion. His real hope was that people would pay more than $35 per share.

On the day of the IPO, lots of people were jittery. LinkedIn was only the second large tech company to go public since the dot-com crash a decade earlier (the first was Google) and the first of any social media to do so. Some were still leery of Internet stocks. LinkedIn was not nearly as big or as popular as Facebook. Would it last or would it be a flash in the pan—a short-lived sensation—as so many of the earlier online companies had been?

Hoffman and LinkedIn CEO Jeffrey Weiner (*center*) smile as they watch the price of shares in their company climb at its IPO at the New York Stock Exchange.

Was it really worth $3 billion? How much would people pay for its stock?

Hoffman gambled that his company would do well. When the New York Stock Exchange opened on May 19, 2011, he had raised the price of the initial offering to $45 per share. As soon as trading began, the price shot up. Over the course of the first day, it more than doubled as people were willing to pay $94.25 for a single share. At the end of the first day of trading, the value of LinkedIn was not $3 billion; it was $9 billion.

LinkedIn was not the only winner that day. Hoffman sold a small portion of his own stock in the company—"less than 1 percent"—and made $5.2 million. That gave him the personal funds to pursue another passion: investing in enterprises that make the world a better place.

CHAPTER 6

Beyond LinkedIn

It was in college that Hoffman first put into words the philosophy that would become the driving force in his life. At that time, he later told *Venture Capital Journal*, he decided that what he wanted to do was "help make a notable contribution to society." By "notable" he meant big—on the scale of affecting at least a million people. By "contribution" he meant something that had a decidedly positive impact. He tried to accomplish that goal through business start-ups—first SocialNet, then PayPal, and then LinkedIn. When he struck it rich with the PayPal sale, he had the means to pursue the same goal through a different path: investing.

ANGEL INVESTOR

When he became a multimillionaire, Hoffman began looking for places where his money would do some good and bring him profits at the same time. The first one he selected was Nanosolar, a company with a revolutionary idea for

Hoffman receives the 2012 Angel of the Year trophy at the Crunchies Awards ceremony. The Crunchies are annual awards given to honor the most exciting start-ups, innovations, and achievements in the technology field.

printing very thin solar panels. Most of the more than eighty companies in which he invested his own money were in the tech field. He was among the first to put money into Friendster, one of the first successful social networks. He helped start Flickr, a site for sharing photos; Six Apart, which provides tools for writing blogs; Zynga, creator of the popular *Farmville* and *Mafia Wars* games; and Digg, a news site to which users contribute content.

Hoffman picked a number of winners. When Mark Zuckerberg was trying to get Facebook off the ground, Hoffman introduced him to his friend Peter Thiel, who led the first round of investment in the then-unknown networking site. Hoffman put in $40,000 of his own, a relatively tiny amount for an Internet investment. When Facebook went public in 2012, Hoffman's small sum was worth $375 million.

Although Hoffman seemed to have a knack for spotting likely successes, he lost money on a few and missed some others. Making money by picking winners was actually his secondary aim as an angel investor. His real love was helping and nurturing people and ideas that would make the world a better place. He did more than contribute money to entrepreneurs he thought were onto something promising. He helped them think through their business plans, plot their companies' growth, and secure additional financing. When a PayPal friend cofounded YouTube, Hoffman gave him an office in the LinkedIn building.

Who Pays for Start-ups?

Venture capitalists, angel investors, and microfinanciers all help new businesses get started and grow.

Venture capitalists and angel investors venture, or risk, their money in the hope they will receive a good return on their investment. They invest in enterprises that look like they have the potential for high profits, which means they are risky and have the potential to fail. Their investment is not a loan that needs to be paid back; it is a purchase of stock that they hope will be worth big money some day.

Venture capitalists (VCs) typically do not invest less than $1 million at a time. Their money comes from many sources and goes into a pool, so they have large amounts of cash. VCs manage the combined funds of many investors.

Angels invest their own money. They are often individuals, but there are some angel investment groups. They have less money than VCs, so they invest in smaller amounts; the average angel investment is under $500,000.

Microfinanciers invest in small (micro) businesses. They lend money to people who are poor who have ideas for starting and building businesses. Microfinanciers deal in very small sums; the investment is a loan. Their motivation is not big profits; it is helping low-income or no-income people become self-sufficient.

In general, Internet start-ups take five years or more to become profitable. Many do not make big money until they go public or are bought by a bigger company. By 2009, a number of the businesses in which Hoffman had invested had paid off for him, which allowed him to continue investing. He had become one of the most successful and sought-after tech investors ever. He also had a reputation as Silicon Valley's "King of Connections," the guy who could link an aspiring entrepreneur with the just-right person who could further an idea or a company. That reputation took him to a new position: venture capitalist.

VENTURE CAPITALIST

In November 2009, Hoffman joined the venture capitalist firm Greylock Partners. As a partner, he was one of a few people deciding where to spend $575 million that investors had entrusted to the partnership. His specialties were tech companies and any innovative enterprises that looked like they could attract millions of users. Of all the VCs, Hoffman chose to work for Greylock for two reasons. One was that he already had relationships with some of the company's partners and, as the LinkedIn tagline says, relationships matter. The

other was that Greylock not only made huge investments, but it also managed smaller amounts for angel investors.

Hoffman could continue making his own angel investments, directing them through Greylock.

Hoffman understood the value of small amounts
of funding as well as giant infusions of capital. Some

Hoffman poses here in his office at Greylock Partners. Greylock is located in San
Francisco, about 30 miles (48 km) from his LinkedIn office in Mountain View.

entrepreneurs need seed money—just enough to do some research or build a prototype so that they can show a bigger investor their product's potential. Greylock put Hoffman in charge of its $20 million Discovery Fund, which is exclusively for seed money and angel investing. Discovery Fund investments are in amounts between $25,000 and $500,000.

Greylock was the perfect place for Hoffman. It enabled him to continue working full-time at LinkedIn and search out and cultivate new ideas at the same time. It let him expand his network of relationships and keep up on the latest developments in the tech world. In addition

to his Discovery Fund activities, Hoffman was involved in Greylock investments in Groupon, an online coupon service; Shopkick, Cyriac Roeding's mobile shopping app; Airbnb, a vacation rental site; Mozilla, creator of the Firefox browser; and several others.

Part of the job of venture capitalists is to serve on the boards of the companies they

In this photograph, Cyriac Roeding appears in his first U.S. job as founder and vice president of CBS Mobile. Hoffman encouraged Roeding to start Shopkick, the largest mobile shopping app in the United States.

help fund. Hoffman spent many hours on corporation boards, sharing information,

A Successful One-Minute Pitch

It was 2006, and Hoffman had resigned from many of the nonprofit boards on which he had served. But, according to an interview with Hoffman, he told a friend he wanted to find something worthwhile to devote some time and money to. His friend asked if he had heard of Kiva. He hadn't, so he looked up the organization on the Web. *That's really cool*, he thought. *I'd love to do that*. But Hoffman worked through relationships, and no one in his sphere was connected with Kiva. Two weeks later, he ran into an old friend, one of the PayPal Mafia: Premal Shah. Shah wanted to talk to him about a great nonprofit. Hoffman braced himself for another pitch; he was always willing to listen to a friend's idea. But when Shah said the nonprofit was Kiva, Hoffman stopped him. "Yes," he blurted out enthusiastically. "Whatever the question that you're about to ask is, the answer is yes."

Shah was surprised. He had heard that Hoffman was saying no to all invitations to join nonprofits. But Kiva met all Hoffman's criteria: it was big, unique, and sustainable. More important, it was making an impact for good on a grand scale. Shah introduced his friend to Kiva's CEO, and Hoffman has been an ardent supporter ever since.

insight, advice, and names of contacts. Another part of the job is to sort through the piles of pitches—requests for funding—that flooded his phone, e-mail, and LinkedIn in-boxes nearly nonstop. It was hectic, morning till night, seven days a week, except for Saturday nights, which he reserved for dates with his wife. Yet he had time for more.

PHILANTHROPIST

What Hoffman had achieved in the business world, he wanted to do in the nonprofit community. He wanted to have a large-scale impact for good in places of need, to invest in organizations in which he could really make a difference. He was not looking for a return on his investment; he wanted to donate his time and money. He sincerely believed what he said often: everyone should do something that's not for oneself every day.

Hoffman was particularly interested in organizations that encourage entrepreneurship. He has given money and served on the boards of several. One is DoSomething, a national movement that develops entrepreneurial thinking and skills in young people as it helps them develop projects that benefit their communities. DoSomething's goal of engaging five million active members by 2015 is of a size that pleases Hoffman.

Hoffman was on the founding board of an even larger national enterprise: the Start-up America Partnership. The partnership is a national organization begun in January 2011 in which corporations, universities, and business leaders pool their expertise and resources to help young companies grow. In its first year

One month after the release of his book, *The Start-up of You*, in February 2012, a San Francisco television reporter interviews Hoffman about the book.

of operation, it had collected more than $1 billion. Like DoSomething, Start-up America has a mission and a scale that Hoffman likes.

On a smaller but growing scale is a program that recruits intelligent and motivated high school students from low-income households and gives them the help and resources to attend some of the best colleges and universities in the country. Questbridge mentors thousands of young people each year, following them from high school through college to their first job after college or graduate school. Some of the fortunate students attend Stanford, Hoffman's alma mater. Hoffman is chairman of the organization's West Coast Advisory Board.

Hoffman's philanthropy is not confined to the United States. He is also involved with two organizations that support international entrepreneurship. He is on the board of Endeavor Global, which is involved in South and Central America and other parts of the world where economies are struggling. Its mission is to find entrepreneurs who are doing great things with few resources and help them grow their businesses. Hoffman is heavily involved in Kiva, a microfinance organization that lends money and provides some technical assistance to people in poor parts of the world so that they can start and grow their own businesses.

Hoffman does more than donate to these causes; he also encourages others to participate. Take Kiva, for example. The program works by connecting donors with the people who have ideas for businesses but no resources to get them started. Kiva checks the people out, making sure they have a good chance to succeed if they are given funds. It lists all the people waiting for business start-up loans, and donors select the people they want their money to go to. Donors can follow the entrepreneurs' progress. What Hoffman did was give $1 million to Kiva and invite anyone who visited the organization's Web site to choose a recipient and loan $25 of his million to that person. His aim was to have forty thousand people use his money to discover the joy of "doing something that's not for yourself" and then invest again on their own. At least forty thousand places on Earth and forty thousand people would be better because of his donation.

MAKING THE WORLD A BETTER PLACE

That is and always has been Hoffman's ultimate goal: he would leave the world a better place. That philosophy of life is what was behind his college dream of becoming a public intellectual. His desire to make the world not just better but massively better caused him to shift to pursue a career in the Internet industry. It was and is the motivation behind all his business ventures, his investment decisions, and his charitable giving. It is the driving force that set LinkedIn apart from other social and professional networks.

Hoffman speaks at the MIT Media Lab, an innovative program of the Massachusetts Institute of Technology that studies the impact of new technologies on everyday life.

Hoffman has largely achieved his goal. More than 175 million people in two hundred countries use the services of LinkedIn. Many give glowing testimonies of how the company has helped them make important connections, find jobs, or expand their businesses. Hundreds of people have started enterprises that reach millions because Hoffman has helped them with funding and advice. Thousands of low-income students graduate from top-notch universities and millions of young people find ways to serve their neighborhoods through programs Hoffman helps support. People all over the globe are raising themselves and their communities to heights they had not dreamed possible because someone in California believes passionately that all people should do something that's not for themselves. Society is definitely a better place because Reid Hoffman has "been there."

Fact Sheet on

REID HOFFMAN

Full Name: Reid Garrett Hoffman

Date of Birth: August 5, 1967

Birthplace: Stanford, California

Education: Stanford University, B.A. in symbolic systems, 1990; Oxford University, M.S. in philosophy, 1993

Current Residence: Palo Alto, California

Family: Married to Michelle Yee, no children

Early Jobs: Apple, Fujitsu, PayPal, and SocialNet

Employment: Chairman, LinkedIn; partner, Greylock Partners

Net Worth: $1.8 billion (according to *Forbes*, March 2012)

Investments: Multiple

Honors/Awards: Marshall Scholarship, Dinklespiel Award, Matthew Arnold Memorial Prize (Proxime Accessit), SD Forum Visionary Award, Henry Crown Fellowship

Boards: Endeavor Global, Globant, Kiva, Mozilla, Questbridge, Shopkick, Tagged, Winster, Wrapp, Zynga

Publications: *Borderlands* (RuneQuest), 1982 (coauthor) *The Start-up of You: Adapt to the Future, Invest in Yourself, and Transform Your Career*, 2012 (coauthor with Ben Casnocha)

Fact Sheet on

LinkedIn

Date Founded: December 2002

Date Launched: May 5, 2003

IPO: May 19, 2011; shares, originally priced at $45, closed at $94.25

Founded by: Reid Hoffman, Allen Blue, Konstantin Guericke, Eric Ly, Jean-Luc Vaillant

Mission: Connecting the world's professionals to make them more productive and successful

Tagline: "Relationships matter"

Revenue: $522 million in 2011

Revenue Sources: Hiring solutions, marketing solutions, premium subscriptions

Net Worth: $9 billion at IPO, May 2011

Members: More than 175 million and growing at a rate of two per second

Employees: 2,861

Headquarters: Mountain View, California

Languages: Seventeen languages: English, Czech, Dutch, French, German, Indonesian, Italian, Japanese, Korean, Malay, Polish, Portuguese, Romanian, Russian, Spanish, Swedish, and Turkish

U.S. Offices: Chicago, Los Angeles, New York, Omaha, San Francisco

International Offices: 20 cities

Scope: More than 200 countries and territories; 62 percent of members are outside the United States

Timeline

August 5, 1967 Reid Garrett Hoffman is born in Stanford, California.

1982–1985 Hoffman attends the Putney School in rural Vermont.

1985–1990 Hoffman attends Stanford University, graduating with a B.S. in symbolic systems and cognitive science.

1990–1993 Hoffman attends Oxford University, graduating with an M.A. in philosophy.

1994 Hoffman begins work at Apple Computer, Inc.

1996 Hoffman begins work at Fujitsu Software Systems.

Summer 1997 Hoffman founds SocialNet.com.

January 2000 Hoffman leaves SocialNet, joins PayPal full-time as executive vice president.

February 15, 2002 PayPal goes public.

October 3, 2002 eBay acquires PayPal for $1.5 billion, making Hoffman and some others multimillionaires.

December 2002 Hoffman cofounds LinkedIn with four friends.

May 5, 2003 LinkedIn cofounders send invitations, launching LinkedIn.

October 2003 In Series A financing, Sequoia Capital invests $4.7 million in LinkedIn.

2004 Hoffman marries college sweetheart, Michelle Yee, in a small ceremony before a justice of the peace and three witnesses.

October 2004 In Series B financing, Greylock invests $10 million in LinkedIn.

March 2005 LinkedIn introduces its first premium paid subscription services.

August 2005 Hoffman becomes a member of the board of directors of Mozilla.

March 2006 LinkedIn becomes profitable.

June 2006 Hoffman becomes a member of the board of directors of Kiva.

January 2007 In Series C financing, Bessemer Venture Partners and European Founders Fund invest $12.8 million in LinkedIn.

February 2007–January 2009 Dan Nye serves as CEO of LinkedIn. Hoffman moves from CEO to position of chairman and president, and takes charge of product development.

March 2007 LinkedIn opens its first office outside Silicon Valley, in Omaha, Nebraska.

October 2007 LinkedIn membership in Great Britain reaches one million.

2008 LinkedIn opens its first office outside the United States, in London, England.

March 2008 Hoffman begins serving on the board of Zynga.

June 2008 In Series D fund-raising, Bain Capital Ventures invests $53 million in LinkedIn.

September 2008 Hoffman accepts chairman position of the West Coast Advisory Board of Questbridge.

October 2008 In continued Series D fund-raising, Goldman Sachs, McGraw-Hill, and SAP Ventures invest $22.7 million in LinkedIn.

December 2008 Dipchand "Deep" Nishar, a director at Google, is hired as LinkedIn's vice president of product (to begin January 2009) and Hoffman returns to position of CEO.

June 2009 Jeff Weiner, an executive vice president of Yahoo!, becomes CEO of LinkedIn; Hoffman becomes executive chairman.

November 2009 Hoffman becomes a partner in venture capital firm Greylock.

May 19, 2011 LinkedIn makes its IPO. Shares, originally priced at $45, close at $94.25.

February 14, 2012 The book *The Start-up of You: Adapt to the Future, Invest in Yourself, and Transform Your Career*, written by Reid Hoffman and Ben Casnocha, is released.

September 2012 *Forbes* lists Hoffman's wealth at $2.1 billion and ranks him as the two hundred and twenty-ninth richest person in America.

Glossary

alma mater Literally "bountiful mother"; the school from which a person graduated.

angel investor An individual who puts money into a young or just-starting business in return for a specified share (usually in stocks) of the future profits of that business if the business becomes profitable.

application A software program run on a computer or other electronic device that has a specific use, or application.

avatar An image or other graphic representation of a computer user.

beta The second phase of testing a software product that is done with a small group of users before releasing of the product to the general public.

blogger A person who writes a journal of his or her opinions on a Web site and updates the journal regularly.

browser Software that enables computer users to locate and retrieve information on the Web.

camaraderie A feeling of closeness and fun among friends.

CEO Chief executive officer; the person in charge of making the decisions for running a company.

chargeback A refund that a credit card company gives to a credit card holder when the holder disputes a particular charge.

cyber- Prefix meaning related to computers or computer networks.

digital Technically relating to information stored in a certain form, but generally used to refer to anything having to do with information stored on computers or other electronic devices.

domain name A string of letters, numbers, or words that is used to locate an organization or other entity on the Web; a Web site's address.

dot-com A company that does all or almost all of its business on the Internet through a Web site.

encryption The process of converting data into a form that cannot be understood except by the person who has the decoding key.

entrepreneur A person who creates and operates a business, taking the financial risk for whether the business succeeds.

IPO Initial public offering; the procedure by which a privately owned company allows the public to purchase shares of the company. The company decides how many shares to offer and how much each will cost.

Mac Short for Macintosh, a computer made by the Apple Corporation.

microfinance The provision of financial services, usually loans of small amounts of money, to people who are not able to obtain money any other way so that they can start small businesses.

PC A personal computer; usually a computer that uses a Windows-based operating system to distinguish it from a computer using a system designed by Apple.

philanthropist A person who gives money, usually through charities, to help people.

platform A computer system or a set of technologies on which application programs can be run.

preppy A person who is or acts like a student from an expensive school and who wears expensive clothes and is concerned mostly with superficial matters.

professional Pertaining to an occupation that requires knowledge and skills that are usually acquired through formal education.

prototype An original model of a new product, often in very simple but working form.

recession A period of significant decline in economic activity lasting six months or longer.

regulatory Having to do with laws or rules that govern how something operates. A regulatory agency is usually a government body that establishes rules for certain types of businesses.

seed money The first money invested to get a company started. Seed money is usually a small amount put into a company at the idea stage, often by the company's owner or family and friends.

Silicon Valley The name given to the southern part of the San Francisco Bay Area, where many computer and electronics companies are located. The name comes from the fact that the area manufactures chips made of silicon for use in technology products.

software Programs, codes, procedures, and other information used to operate computers and other electronic devices.

tagline An advertising phrase that communicates the vision of a company in a brief way; slogan.

venture capitalist A person or company that invests money in a new business to help it get started or help it expand, usually in exchange for a share in the profits of the business.

virtual Similar to reality but not actually real. Computers can create virtual objects that look like the objects they simulate.

For More Information

Bloomberg L.P.
Bloomberg Tower
731 Lexington Avenue
New York, NY 10022
(212) 318-2000 (East Coast); (415) 912- 2960 (West
Coast)
Web site: http://www.bloomberg.com
Bloomberg provides business and financial data, news,
analysis, and insight via a variety of media including
magazines, television, Web sites, and books.

Canada Federation of Independent Business
401-4141 Yonge Street
Toronto, ON M2P 2A6
Canada
(416) 222-8022; (888) 234-2232
and
1202-99 Metcalfe Street
Ottawa, ON K1P 6L7
Canada
(613) 235-2373; (888) 234-2232

Web site: http://www.cfib-fcei.ca

This federation represents the interests of small business owners to national, regional, and local governments, and provides research and information to businesses.

Canadian Youth Business Foundation

100 Adelaide Street West, Suite 1302

Toronto, ON M5H 1S3

Canada

(866) 646-2922

(800) 464-2923

Web site: http://cybf.ca

This foundation helps aspiring entrepreneurs ages eighteen to thirty-four advance their business ideas from prelaunch through start-up and implementation by providing information, coaching, access to start-up and expansion funding, and other resources.

DoSomething

(212) 254-2390

Web site: http://www.dosomething.org

This national nonprofit organization encourages teens to do something to make meaningful, positive differences in their communities, and it organizes campaigns and provides resources so that they can.

Endeavor Global

900 Broadway, # 301

New York, NY 10003

(212) 352-3200

Web site: http://www.endeavor.org

Endeavor is a movement that enables and supports economic development around the world by mentoring and helping entrepreneurs.

Greylock Partners

2550 Sand Hill Road, Suite 200

Menlo Park, CA 94025

(650) 493-5525

and

One Brattle Square, 4th floor

Cambridge, MA 02138

(781) 622-2200

Web site: http://www.greylock.com

An investment company established in 1965, Greylock extends seed, early investment, and growth funds to entrepreneurs in the tech field.

International Council for Small Business

George Washington University School of Business

Funger Hall, Suite 315

2201 G Street NW

Washington, DC 20052

(202) 994-6380

Web site: http://www.icsb.org

This membership organization was established in
1955 and includes researchers, educators, government officials, businesses, and trade associations
that provide information and contacts to promote
the growth and development of small business
worldwide.

Kiva Microfunds

875 Howard Street, Suite #340

San Francisco, CA 94103

(828) 479-5482

Web site: http://www.kiva.org

Kiva is a microfinance organization that lends funds to
aspiring entrepreneurs in poor regions of the world so
that they can create businesses.

PayPal

2211 North First Street

San Jose, CA 95131

Web site: http://www.paypal.com

PayPal is an online company that allows people to
exchange money without sharing their financial
information.

Questbridge

115 Everett Avenue

Palo Alto, CA 94301

(650) 331-3280

(888) 275-2054

Web site: http://www.questbridge.org

This nonprofit organization places talented low-income youth into twenty-eight top colleges and mentors them so that they will be successful.

WEB SITES

Due to the changing nature of Internet links, Rosen Publishing has developed an online list of Web sites related to the subject of this book. This site is updated regularly. Please use this link to access the list:

http://www.rosenlinks.com/IBIO/Link

For Further Reading

Anandra, Mitra. *Digital Communications: From E-Mail to the Cyber Community.* New York, NY: Chelsea House Publishers, 2010.

Anderson, Jennifer Joline. *Wikipedia: The Company and Its Founder.* San Francisco, CA: Essential Library, 2011.

Baber, Anne, and Lynne Waymon. *Make Your Contacts Count: Networking Know-how for Business and Career Success.* New York, NY: Amacom, 2007.

Brandt, Richard. *The Google Guys: Inside the Brilliant Minds of Google Founders Larry Page and Sergey Brin.* New York, NY: Portfolio/Penguin, 2009.

Brezina, Corona. *Sergey Brin, Larry Page, Eric Schmidt, and Google.* New York, NY: Rosen Publishing, 2013.

Bryfonski, Dedria, ed. *Global Impact of Social Media.* Detroit, MI: Greenhaven Press, 2011.

Dobinick, Susan. *Mark Zuckerberg and Facebook.* New York, NY: Rosen Publishing, 2013.

Fox, Scott. *Internet Riches: The Simple Money-Making Secrets of Online Millionaires.* New York, NY: Amacom, 2008.

Hafner, Katie, and Matthew Lyon. *Where Wizards Stay Up Late: The Origins of the Internet.* New York, NY: Simon & Schuster, 2006.

Hamon, Susan. *Google: The Company and Its Founders.* San Francisco, CA: Essential Library, 2011.

Kirk, Amanda. *Internet and Media: An All-In-One Guide to Navigating Toward a New Career.* New York, NY: Ferguson, 2009.

Kirkpatrick, David. *The Facebook Effect: The Inside Story of the Company That Is Connecting the World.* New York, NY: Simon & Schuster, 2010.

Landau, Jennifer. *Jeff Bezos and Amazon.* New York, NY: Rosen Publishing, 2013.

Lusted, Marcia Amidon. *Apple: The Company and Its Visionary Founder, Steve Jobs.* San Francisco, CA: Essential Library, 2012.

Meyer, Jared. *Making Friends: The Art of Social Networking in Life and Online.* New York, NY: Rosen Publishing, 2011.

Meyer, Susan. *Jimmy Wales and Wikipedia.* New York, NY: Rosen Publishing, 2013.

Perry, Chris. *LinkedUp: The Ultimate LinkedIn Job Search Guide.* Seattle, WA; CreateSpace, 2011.

Porterfield, Jason. *Julian Assange and Wikileaks.* New York, NY: Rosen Publishing, 2013.

Qualman, Erik. *Socialnomics: How Social Media Transforms the Way We Live and Do Business.* Rev. ed. Hoboken, NJ: Wiley, 2011.

Rowell, Rebecca. *YouTube: The Company and Its Founders.* San Francisco, CA: Essential Library, 2011.

Shea, Therese. *Steve Jobs and Apple.* New York, NY: Rosen Publishing, 2013.

Stenzel, Pam, and Melissa Nesdahl. *Who's In Your Social Network?: Understanding the Risks Associated with Modern Media and Social Networking and How It Can Impact Your Character and Relationships.* Ventura, CA: Regal, 2012.

Taylor, Allan. *Career Opportunities in the Internet, Video Games, and Multimedia.* New York, NY: Checkmark, 2007.

Wilkinson, Colin. *Going Live: Launching Your Digital Business.* New York, NY: Rosen Publishing, 2012.

Wolny, Philip. *Andrew Mason and Groupon.* New York, NY: Rosen Publishing, 2013.

Bibliography

Aragon, Lawrence. "Reid Hoffman Interview by *Venture Capital Journal*" (video). 2010. Retrieved May 2, 2012 (http://www.pehub.com/105903/video-1-on-1-with-reid-hoffman-the-mastermind-behind-linkedin).

Baldwin, Clare, and Alina Selyukh. "LinkedIn Share Price More Than Doubles in NYSE Debut." *New York Times*, May 19, 2011. Retrieved July 21, 2012 (http://www.reuters.com/article/2011/05/19/us-linkedin-ipo-risks-idUSTRE74H0TL20110519).

Bloomberg Game Changers. "Reid Hoffman Revealed" (video). Retrieved May 23, 2012 (http://www.bloomberg.com/video/92790093-reid-hoffman-revealed-bloomberg-game-changers.html).

Couts, Andrew. "LinkedIn: 6.5 Million Encrypted Passwords Leaked as iOS App Comes Under Fire [Update: LinkedIn Confirms Breach]." *Digital Trends,* June 6, 2012. Retrieved July 26, 2012 (http://www.digitaltrends.com/social-media/linkedin-6-5-million-passwords-leaked-as-ios-app-comes-under-fire).

Eskin, Blake. "Like Monopoly in the Depression, Settlers of Catan Is the Board Game of Our Time." *Washington Post*, November 21, 2010.

Guericke, Konstantin. "How LinkedIn Broke
    Through." ZURB Soapbox podcast,
    September 8, 2010. Retrieved June 25, 2012
    (http://www.zurb.com/soapbox/events/8/
    Konstantin-Guericke-ZURBsoapbox).

Hoffman, Reid, as told to Ellen Lee. "LinkedIn's
    Startup Story: Connecting the Business World."
    CNN Money, June 2, 2009. Retrieved April 26, 2012
    (http://money.cnn.com/2009/06/02/smallbusiness/
    linkedin_startup_story.smb).

Hoffman, Reid, as told to Mark Lacter. "How I Did
    It: Reid Hoffman of LinkedIn." *Inc.*, May 1, 2009.
    Retrieved May 2, 2012 (http://www.inc.com/
    magazine/20090501/how-i-did-it-reid-hoffman
    -of-linkedin.html).

Hoffman, Reid, and Ben Casnocha. *The Start-up of
    You: Adapt to the Future, Invest in Yourself, and
    Transform Your Career.* New York, NY: Crown
    Business, 2012.

Horgan, Richard. "History of LinkedIn." *Sophisticated
    Edge.* Retrieved June 16, 2012 (http://www
    .sophisticatededge.com/history-of-linkedin.html).

LinkedIn. "About." Retrieved July 23, 2012 (http://press
    .linkedin.com/about).

LinkedIn. "LinkedIn Announces First Quarter 2012
    Financial Results." May 3, 2012. Retrieved July 28,
    2012 (http://press.linkedin.com/node/1192).

LinkedIn. "LinkedIn Launches Premium Service
for Recruiters and Researchers." August 8, 2005.
Retrieved July 26, 2012 (http://press.linkedin.com/76/
linkedin-launches-premium-service-recruiters-and
-researchers).

LinkedIn. "LinkedIn Launches Relationship-Powered
Job Network." March 1, 2005. Retrieved July 26, 2012
(http://press.linkedin.com/75/linkedin-launches
-relationship-powered-job-network).

LinkedIn. "LinkedIn Launches Two New Subscription
Offerings." November 22, 2005. Retrieved July 26,
2012 (http://press.linkedin.com/77/linkedin
-launches-two-new-subscription-offerings).

LinkedIn. "Reid Hoffman." Retrieved May 2, 2012
(http://www.linkedin.com/in/reidhoffman).

Los Altos Town Crier. "William Parker Hoffman, Obituary."
October 19, 2010. Retrieved April 26, 2012 (http://
www.losaltosonline.com/index.php?option=com_
content&task=view&id=22452&Itemid=54).

O'Brien, Jeffrey M. "Meet the PayPal Mafia." *Fortune,*
November 26, 2007. Retrieved June 7, 2012
(http://money.cnn.com/2007/11/13/magazines/
fortune/paypal_mafia.fortune/index.htm).

PayPal Press Center. "History." Retrieved June 6, 2012
(https://www.paypal-media.com/history).

Rowan, David. "For LinkedIn Founder Reid Hoffman,
Relationships Rule the World," *Wired,* March 20,

2010. Retrieved April 30, 2012 (http://www.wired
.com/epicenter/2012/03/ff_hoffman/all/1).

Rusli, Evelyn M. "A King of Connections Is Tech's
Go-To Guy." *New York Times Business Day*,
November 5, 2011. Retrieved May 5, 2012
(http://www.nytimes.com/2011/11/06/business/
reid-hoffman-of-linkedin-has-become-the-go-to
-guy-of-tech.html?pagewanted=all).

San Jose Mercury News. "Louise May Hoffman,
Obituary." June 19, 2011. Retrieved April 26, 2012
(http://www.legacy.com/obituaries/mercurynews/
obituary.aspx?n=louise-hoffman&pid=152061404).

Stern, Michael. "Who Owns Facebook?" *Massinvestor,
Inc.* Retrieved July 21, 2010 (http://whoowns
facebook.com).

Wilson, Stephen. *Social Media and Small Business
Marketing.* Seattle, WA; CreateSpace, 2010.

Index

ABOUT THE AUTHOR

After living twelve years in Silicon Valley, Ann Byers now resides in Fresno, California. A youth worker, editor, and author, she has written, among other books, biographies of Jaime Escalante, Neil Armstrong, Oskar Schindler, and Jeffrey Bezos.

PHOTO CREDITS

Designer: Brian Garvey; Editor: Kathy Kuhtz Campbell; Photo Researcher: Karen Huang